Pebble® Plus

Looking at Animal Parts

Let's Look at Animal Eyes

by Wendy Perkins

Consulting Editor: Gail Saunders-Smith, PhD

Consultant: Suzanne B. McLaren, Collections Manager
Section of Mammals, Carnegie Museum of Natural History
Edward O'Neil Research Center, Pittsburgh, Pennsylvania

Capstone press®

Mankato, Minnesota

Pebble Plus is published by Capstone Press,
151 Good Counsel Drive, P.O. Box 669, Mankato, Minnesota 56002.
www.capstonepress.com

1 2 3 4 5 6 11 10 09 08 07 06

Library of Congress Cataloging-in-Publication Data
Perkins, Wendy, 1957–
    Let's look at animal eyes / by Wendy Perkins.
    p. cm.—(Pebble plus. Looking at animal parts)
    Summary: "Simple text and photographs present animal eyes, how they work, and how different animals
use them"—Provided by publisher.
    Includes bibliographical references and index.
    ISBN-13: 978-0-7368-6349-0 (hardcover)
    ISBN-10: 0-7368-6349-4 (hardcover)
    1. Eye—Juvenile literature. I. Title. II. Series.
QL949.P47 2007
591.4′4—dc22   2006000997

Editorial Credits
Sarah L. Schuette, editor; Kia Adams, set designer; Renée Doyle, cover production; Kelly Garvin, photo
    researcher/photo editor

Photo Credits
Brand X Pictures, cover
Dwight R. Kuhn, 14–15
James P. Rowan, 11
McDonald Wildlife Photography/Joe McDonald, 6–7
Minden Pictures/Frans Lanting, 4–5
Nature Picture Library/Carine Schrurs, 8–9; Gertrud & Helmut Denzau, 18–19; Peter Scoones, 16–17
Pete Carmichael, 1
Peter Arnold/John Cancalosi, 12–13
Shutterstock/pixelman, 21

Note to Parents and Teachers

The Looking at Animal Parts set supports national science standards related to life
science. This book describes and illustrates animal eyes. The images support early readers
in understanding the text. The repetition of words and phrases helps early readers learn
new words. This book also introduces early readers to subject-specific vocabulary words,
which are defined in the Glossary section. Early readers may need assistance to read
some words and to use the Table of Contents, Glossary, Read More, Internet Sites, and
Index sections of the book.

Table of Contents

Eyes at Work

Animals see the world
with their eyes.
Some animals see color.
Other animals see black,
white, and gray.

Pupils let light into the eye.

Animals with large pupils

can see well at night.

A lion squints and stares
at a herd of zebras.
It picks out the best one
to chase.

The zebra looks around
for danger.
It sees the lion sneaking up
from behind. Run!

Kinds of Eyes

Chameleons have two eyes

that move alone.

One looks in front.

The other looks to the side.

Flies have hundreds of eyes
that work together.
Each eye sees part
of the same picture.

Alligators open their

eyes wide underwater.

Two sets of eyelids

keep water out.

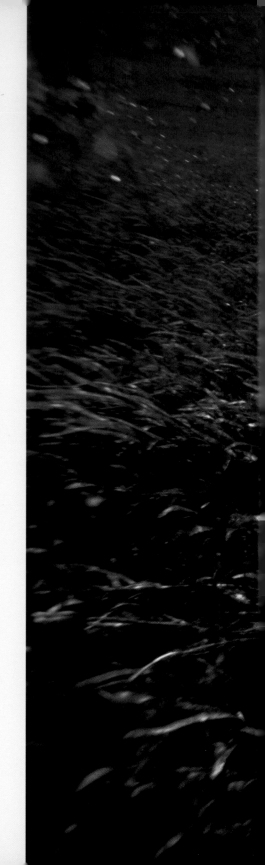

Camels can still see
during sand storms.
Long eyelashes keep
sand out of their eyes.

Awesome Animal Eyes

Looking or watching,
animals use their eyes
in many ways.

Glossary

eyelash—one of the curved hairs that grows on the edge of each eyelid

eyelid—the upper or lower fold of skin that covers the eye when it is closed

herd—a large group of animals that live and move together

pupil—the round black part of the eye that lets light travel through it

squint—to nearly close the eye in order to see something better

Read More

Hall, Kirsten. *Animal Sight.* Animals and Their Senses. Milwaukee: Weekly Reader Early Learning Library, 2006.

Hall, Peg. *Whose Eyes Are These?: A Look At Animal Eyes—Big, Round, and Narrow.* Whose Is It? Minneapolis: Picture Window Books, 2003.

Miles, Elizabeth. *Eyes.* Animal Parts. Chicago: Heinemann Library, 2003.

Internet Sites

FactHound offers a safe, fun way to find Internet sites related to this book. All of the sites on FactHound have been researched by our staff.

Here's how:

1. Visit *www.facthound.com*

2. Choose your grade level.

3. Type in this book ID **07368663494** for age-appropriate sites. You may also browse subjects by clicking on letters, or by clicking on pictures and words.

4. Click on the **Fetch It** button.

FactHound will fetch the best sites for you!

23

Index

Word Count: 137
Grade: 1
Early-Intervention Level: 14